AS A PRISONER THINKETH

OTHER BOOKS BY CARL B. BROCK

Chains & Things

The Underground Credit Builder's Handbook

The Seven Ways to Overcome the Federal Statute of Limitations

AS A PRISONER THINKETH

Carl B. Brock

© Copyright 2015 by Carl B. Brock

All Rights Reserved.

www.AsAPrisonerThinketh.com

The text of this book may be quoted without permission in any form (written, electronic, audio, etc.) as long as no more than 25 percent of the total text of the book is quoted.

ISBN: 978-0-6927157-8-9

DISCLAIMER

While this is a work of nonfiction, all original names and places have been changed to protect the identities and reputations of the actual persons and events this work is based on. Any resemblance to actual persons with the changed names and places used in this work is entirely coincidental and should be considered as such.

CONTENTS

Introduction	i
Redefining Your Legacy	1
Be a True Leader	5
Know What You Stand For	9
Maintaining Meaningful Relationships	13
Naysayers, Dream Killers, and Distraction Devices	19
Keeping Your Word	25
The Lonely Road	31
Mastering Your Emotions	35
Influence	39
Learning How To Trust	43
Overlook The Small Stuff	51
Taking Action	55
Choose a Direction In Life	59
Life-Changing Events	65

Spiritual Journeys	71
Find A Mentor	75
Hope Keeps the Spirit Alive	81
Results	87
Acknowledgments	89
About The Author	91

"For man is man and master of his fate"

—Lord Alfred Tennyson, *Idylls of the King* (1859)

INTRODUCTION

Achievement, of whatever kind, is the crown of effort, the diadem of thought.

—James Allen, *As a Man Thinketh* (1903)

Hello, reader. My name is Carl. I'd like to thank you for taking the time to give this small book of mine a chance. *As A Prisoner Thinketh* is the product of much thought and consideration and is written from the humble perspective of myself as a prisoner. The title is a tribute to the late author James Allen (1864–1912), as well as a great piece of work that he wrote, *As a Man Thinketh*. I would like to make it

Carl B. Brock

clear that my book is not written as an expansion on Allen's writings, nor would I attempt to compare it to any of those that he wrote.

As A Prisoner Thinketh is a group of essays that I wrote from ideas and thoughts that were inspired while reading and studying works written by authors like Allen and then making conscious observations about myself, life, love, friendship, family, prison, spirituality, and countless other things.

I advise you to read this book with an open mind so that you can appreciate the perspective from which I write: behind the walls of federal prison. I hope and pray that these thoughts of mine can do some good in your life, help you produce worthwhile thoughts, and, if necessary, initiate meaningful change.

I know that this book will meet some resistance along the way because a prisoner wrote it. I am just glad to be able to share it with anyone I can. I think that even if a person does

As A Prisoner Thinketh

not agree with everything I have to say, he or she will be able to at least gain something positive out of the experience.

I wish you all peace and prosperity.

—Carl B. Brock

REDEFINING YOUR LEGACY

"Man is manacled only by himself. Thought and action are the jailers of Fate—they imprison, being base. They are also the angels of Freedom—they liberate, being noble."

—James Allen, *As a Man Thinketh* (1903)

Many people in prison seem to have trouble moving forward with their lives. The reason is, in part, that they put too much stock into their past.

People tend to use past failures and bad decisions as tools of resistance that hamper their ability and resolve to create better lives. Indeed, it is important to know where you came from, just as it is important to accept what you have or have not done, for better or worse. Yet a dark past does not have to set the stage for the future.

As to those in prison who can't seem to move forward, the root of their resistance is typically their willingness to allow their cloudy pasts to define who they are and where they are going. If you were to ask one of these people, "What are you going to do once you get out of prison?" a common response is, "I'll do what I can do, which probably won't be much, considering my criminal record."

It is sad because this statement is both true and false at the same time. If a prisoner holds his criminal record to be his legacy, then indeed, he probably won't do much in life besides more prison time. But if the prisoner were to consider his or her criminal record as a short chapter in a large book, then this type of statement would

As A Prisoner Thinketh

likely prove to be false because a prisoner with this mind-set would probably find the motivation and determination to create a legacy that outshines his or her grim past.

As long as we are alive, we still have time to think, say, or do things differently. While we may have burned bridges, broken hearts, and hurt many people, we can still change. Although we cannot always fix what has been broken or make things the way they used to be, we can still move forward with a positive attitude and make the right choices in the future. The wrongs of our past don't control what we think, say, or do—only we control those things.

For instance, there is a man named Joe. He spent two decades in prison for all sorts of federal crimes. While Joe did his time, he pursued higher knowledge and sought to educate and discipline himself. He taught himself the legal system and informally studied law. It was not long before Joe realized that law was a subject he enjoyed learning and that he had a knack for conducting legal research and drafting court filings.

Joe eventually became what is known as a "jailhouse lawyer." He helped other prisoners work on their criminal cases, file lawsuits for gross injustices, and fill out tedious and complicated forms for matters like estates, trusts, marriages, and divorces. Once Joe got out of prison, he went on to let go of the ways of his past. He started his very own legal research center and now makes an honest and prosperous living as a paralegal. You could say that Joe has found his way. He has created a new and better life for himself despite his past.

A past that we are not proud of does not have to define us and/or where we are going. We can take control of our lives and redefine our legacies. So let me repeat what I said earlier: as long as we are alive, we can change the way we think, the words that come out of our mouths, and the way we act.

BE A TRUE LEADER

"The art of leadership is saying no, not yes.
It is very easy to say yes."

—Tony Blair, *Mail on Sunday* (1994)

Being a true leader is not as hard as it may sound. The first step is to realize that you have the potential to be one. The next step is to choose a direction in which to lead.

I myself have never been a follower, though I was never much of a leader, either. I was like a ship at sea with no captain at the helm: I went where the wind blew but never with much purpose or direction.

Carl B. Brock

I've found from experience that it is not until you know what you stand for and what you want in life that you can determine your direction in life. This is part of what reveals your destination. Once you know these things about yourself and can hold them with confidence and conviction, the choices and decisions you make will begin to point you in a direction.

True leaders know what and who they are. They know where they are going and understand where they are from. This is why a true leader is unlikely to succumb to peer pressure.

Followers, on the other hand, usually have no idea about who they are or what they stand for. Followers are usually content with leaning on someone they perceive as stronger or smarter than themselves, rather than making their own way. True leaders are quite the opposite of followers in this regard because they'd rather follow their own stars, even if it's a lonelier or more difficult route to travel.

As A Prisoner Thinketh

It was not long in life before it dawned on me that I had the potential to become a leader, but it was not until I was many years into my prison sentence before I finally decided who I was and where I actually wanted to go. Once I decided what my principles, belief system, and spirituality were, I knew what I stood for. And once I knew what I stood for, it was a lot easier for me to determine what my goals, ambitions, and aspirations were.

Disorder and chaos are impossible to eliminate, but life becomes more stable and organized when you come to know yourself. Once you know who you are, it seems as though the pathway is lit. Now you have a sense of purpose. Now you have direction. Now you can move forward with confidence and conviction. And you can take my word for it: once you do, there will be plenty of followers.

KNOW WHAT YOU STAND FOR

"Man is a credulous animal, and must believe something; in the absence of good grounds for belief, he will be satisfied with bad ones."

—Bertrand Russell, *Unpopular Essays* (1950)

If you lack confidence or purpose in life, it is probably because you don't know what you stand for.

If you don't know what you stand for, you have no foundation to stand on and thus lack conviction in your choices and decisions. This causes fear, stress, insecurity, and anxiety. To solve this, we must look inside ourselves to find out who we truly are.

The wisdom offered here is for us to individually make conscious observations of the inner workings of our own hearts and minds so that we can refer to them when such life choices and decisions are to be made. Each person needs to acknowledge and define what he or she holds to be true or false and right or wrong. We each have our very own beliefs, spirituality, sense of justice, and honor. Once we figure out what these are, we have our own individual foundation to stand on.

A person who stands on something knows when to stand for something. These things on which we stand are our principles. These principles help form our core beliefs. And these core beliefs are what outline a person's code of ethics. Once we have acknowledged and defined these things in ourselves, we can make choices and decisions with confidence.

As A Prisoner Thinketh

When we know what we stand for, we have a good idea of who we are. This type of person is unlikely to be manipulated or pressured into doing something that he or she will regret later. In fact, the connivers and schemers are likely to look elsewhere for easier prey. A person of principles is not easily misled or enticed—he or she is usually the one who does the leading and influences others. What I am telling you here is to give yourself a certain code to live by. Think of a blackjack dealer in a casino. When the dealer's cards add up to sixteen or less, he will deal him or herself another card without hesitation. Dealers don't have to ask, "Should I?" or "Shouldn't I?" because they play with a never-changing set of rules that were established well before that particular game ever began. As a result, they know what they must do with every hand of cards because these firm rules guide their moves. Therefore, they can play the game with confidence and conviction.

Carl B. Brock

The lesson here is to know what you stand for in order to have something to stand on. And once you do, just like the blackjack dealer does on seventeen or greater, you can stand very strong indeed.

MAINTAINING MEANINGFUL RELATIONSHIPS

"As iron sharpens iron,
so a man sharpens the countenance of his friend
[to show rage or worthy purpose]."

—Proverbs 27:17, *Amplified Bible*

Certain people are not good company; this is why we should avoid being around them. Just as a person can sharpen the countenance of another, so can a person dull another's countenance. Ask yourself: how many of your friends, family, and associates are assisting you in becoming successful? Would you say that any of them are wasting your time and distracting you from maturing intellectually, emotionally, or spiritually?

Think about each person you interact with on a daily or regular basis. Examine the nature of the conversations that you have with each and the substance of the topics about which you talk. Can you honestly say that each is a healthy and meaningful relationship?

Or would you have to admit that there is at least one person who always interrupts your progress and productivity? There may be more than one person in your group who does this. This seems to be a regular problem that many high school and college students have. Rather than surrounding themselves with motivated and goal-oriented pals, they allow their social circles to be full of underachievers.

As A Prisoner Thinketh

Why, in our culture, is it OK to settle for less than one's potential? Why do certain people in society frown on someone for changing or progressing?

In order to achieve greatness, we need to distance ourselves from those who choose less in life. This is a necessary sacrifice that we must accept in order to be able to invest the necessary attention into whatever we want to obtain.

If a person desires little in life, then he or she will naturally associate with these types of people instead of separating him or herself from them. But if you desire what is not common, a type of greatness, then you will need to keep these people at a distance or somehow remove them from your circle. If you allow these kinds of people (see the next chapter, "Naysayers, Dream Killers, and Distraction Devices") to stay in your company, they will likely do everything in their powers to divert you from your goals and progress.

Carl B. Brock

We must understand that some people just don't want better for us or for themselves. If they did, they would help us achieve what we desire and aspire to, rather than slow us down or continuously distract us from our potential.

True leaders neither allow themselves to be led by a lesser person—unless they wish to become lesser—nor lower themselves to other people's levels, especially for the sake of social acceptance. They instead require people to raise their standards to theirs.

If you wish for another to train, assist, or mold you, you must make the necessary changes in yourself so as to help, rather than resist, that person's efforts.

The fool cannot lead the wise, nor can the wise man lead the fool. But the wise can become fools by following the foolish.

Ultimately, we must sharpen each other. I sharpen you, or you sharpen me. If no one is

As A Prisoner Thinketh

being sharpened in the relationship, then someone or both parties are being dulled. And to be dulled is to live below one's potential.

NAYSAYERS, DREAM KILLERS, AND DISTRACTION DEVICES

"Change is not made without inconvenience, even from worse to better."

—Samuel Johnson, A Dictionary of the English Language (1755)

It may sound strange, but at times there are more people than you realize who want you to remain the same you, without progress or change.

Carl B. Brock

I'm not talking about the people who are genuine and want the best for you. I am talking about those who appear to genuinely care for you but actually only care about what is best for them. These people are thus known as Naysayers, Dream Killers, and Distraction Devices.

These disingenuous people want to maintain the status quo. They usually aren't interested in change themselves and definitely don't want to see anyone around them change. My theory as to why is that these people are living their lives based on fears, such as insecurity, apprehension, or uncertainty. Moreover, if you change, the pressure is on for them to change.

Here is a story about two obese men I know named Jim and Zach. They have been friends their whole lives, and then one day Zach decides to take the necessary steps to get healthy and in better physical shape. When Zach does this, it changes the entire nature of their relationship. They go from enjoying the same unhealthy meals and low-energy entertainment to Zach's suddenly eating new, healthier meals and trying out more active forms of recreation. This exposes Zach to new people, new ideas, and new principles.

In turn, the change makes Jim insecure since he's not ready to make any alterations to his life. His insecurity causes him to try to dissuade Zach from his new lifestyle. He uses negative feedback and makes numerous attempts to entice Zach into returning to his old eating habits and lazy leisure activities. Eventually, Zach realizes what is happening and decides to quit spending time with Jim. This scenario happens quite often when a person is trying to improve his or her life. I've seen people respond very negatively to many changes that you would think would prompt encouragement and positive reinforcement. One example would be when a man tries to quit smoking. Or maybe it's a woman trying to save money or get out of debt. In prison, this often happens to someone trying to quit drugs or stop gambling. Another common story in prison is when a guy is trying to understand or pursue his spirituality and religious beliefs. This last scenario typically attracts plenty of misgivings from others, because for various reasons people hate to see someone get so-called jailhouse religion.

There are different kinds of people who try to keep others from changing. There are the Naysayers, who like to sow seeds of doubt and negativity about everything. There are the Dream Killers, who try to convince people that what they want, aspire to, or seek is not possible. And then there are those who act as Distraction Devices, deliberately trying to interfere with a person's progress and productivity.

I have experienced them all. These people want us to remain the same person forever for their own selfish reasons and purposes. Some are subtle with their manipulations, while others are brazen and bold.

I've learned that if you want to progress,

change, or evolve, then you must prepare yourself for resistance. It is the people closest to you who can really cause you the most problems and inconveniences.

The road to change can be a lonely journey. It can be full of pain and heartbreak, especially since people will reveal their true nature to you along the way. Their true colors may turn out to be something that you don't find agreeable. But we must be strong and move forward with confidence and conviction. Nothing is easy in life, especially change, and that is why so few ever achieve it.

Instead of changing with us or supporting our progress and accomplishments, some people in our circles would rather become obstacles in our way. In these situations, we must be firm and assertive. We cannot allow these people to negatively affect our hope or determination. The reality is that we must make the right choices for ourselves, based on what future we want. We must not allow others to distract, manipulate, or cause us to lose our resolve.

True friends or genuine loved ones will support us in our change. They will want us to do better and live healthier. They want us to do what is right and would never try to make us fall or relapse, and they would not try to entice us or influence us in negative ways. Instead, they would encourage our metamorphosis, even if the path we take is not for them, just as we would do for them in return.

But the Naysayers, Dream Killers, and Distraction Devices won't be able to do this: they need us to stay the same. And if we don't separate ourselves from such people, we most likely will stay the same indeed.

KEEPING YOUR WORD

"A man's [moral] self shall be filled with the fruit of his mouth; and with the consequence of his words he must be satisfied [whether good or evil]."

—Proverbs 18:20, *Amplified Bible*

One of the most valuable assets a person can have in life is his or her word. Prisoners, including myself, place a special emphasis on this asset.

There can be a lot of power in a person's word. It can mean everything when the chips are down. It can also be an assurance at efforts in war or peace. If we are known to keep our word, then, obviously, what we say is not to be taken lightly.

On a day-to-day basis in society, credit-rating companies work very hard to evaluate how well a person repays creditors. Notably, a lot of this credit is issued to people in unsecured forms. If the people taking out the loans do not repay this unsecured debt, the creditor takes a financial loss. The people, in return, lose out on future credit opportunities because the companies issuing the credit have lost confidence in the borrowers' ability to keep their end of the deal. People may not think much about it, but this is a form of breaking your word.

In prison, if you borrow something from someone, you do it on the basis of your word. If you fail to fulfill what you said you would do, you have broken that trust.

Sometimes breaking your word can't be helped because unforeseen circumstances can keep you from fulfilling your good intentions.

As A Prisoner Thinketh

Reasonable people will usually understand when you do not keep your word because of unpredictable events that occurred after you gave it, especially if you can show that you did everything in your power to keep it. If you're conscientious and up front, many times there's a way to make up for the inconvenience to the other party so future dealings with this party are not damaged.

Let's use Lance as an example. He's a humble guy who is known in prison for keeping his word and doing good business. The only thing about Lance is that he's in debt with others on a regular basis. However, he does have a decent job in the prison factory and makes good money since he is a hard worker. Lance always pays his debts when he gets his check and has never tried to trick or cheat anyone out of any money.

One day, some time ago, Lance got laid off. When this happened, he owed significant sums of money to some very serious people. Lance, like many Americans, lived from paycheck to paycheck. Naturally, he did not have anything in his savings for a rainy day. Needless to say, poor old Lance was very stressed out. Since he happened to be in a maximum-security prison, you can imagine how not paying off his debts might be harmful to his health.

However, Lance did have a good reputation, and he was wise enough to have only done business with reasonable (albeit serious) people known for making logic-based decisions. Fortunately, Lance was able to work out an arrangement where he cleaned other prisoners' cells, washed and ironed clothes, and did other miscellaneous jobs to pay his bills until he could get back to work.

It was important that Lance had the wisdom to not try to duck or hide from his problems. Instead, he did everything in his power to maintain his word and reputation. Eventually, Lance paid all of his debts in full, and most of

As A Prisoner Thinketh

them were repaid before he even got his job back.

A person who does not keep his word loses respect from others. In some places, such as prison, respect can be the only thing that keeps others at bay. A person with no respect in prison is not taken seriously, and he or she is usually treated badly as well.

If your word is no good, then people won't trust you, and no one will do you any kind of favors. Even when you do tell the truth, no one will believe you. As in the old fable about the boy who cried wolf, you damage your credibility by sounding false alarms about nonexistent wolves. And just like the story, when an actual wolf does appear, no one will come to help you. If you do not keep your word, then it loses credibility, and when you actually need it to be there for you, it won't be. The good thing, though, is that the more you keep your word, the stronger it gets, just as your credit score will improve when you consistently pay your bills on time.

Take your word seriously; it does mean something. Others will know they can depend on you. Your word is a large part of who and what you are.

THE LONELY ROAD

"Everywhere I see bliss, from which
I alone am irrevocably excluded."

—Mary Shelley, *Frankenstein* (1818)

Loneliness is a natural part of human existence. We should expect that there will be moments when we are alone.

I am quite familiar with loneliness. I know how it feels to be in a room full of people and yet still feel like I am the only one there. I think that during such times, we have an opportunity to reflect on and reevaluate our lives. These times can be a chance to test our resolve or, if we allow it, to feed our insecurities.

The more I learn about myself, who I am, and what I believe, the stronger my inner peace becomes.

At first, being alone bothered me. I had to grow used to my own thoughts and company. It was painful at times to be alone. As I've grown older and matured, I've discovered that a person can lean on and entertain him or herself. Now I am quite at ease with my own company in times of solitude: I've learned to be there for myself whenever I am alone.

Loneliness is a powerful emotion. It can, and does, drive people to do things that they might not normally do. It has inspired songs and poetry. It has also pushed people to chronic depression, substance abuse, and suicide. For instance, some people may leave home and travel far because of loneliness, while others may find solace at the bottom of a liquor bottle.

As A Prisoner Thinketh

I think that it's important to understand that we as humans will all experience loneliness at one time or another. The idea I'm expressing here is for it to be a productive part of an ever-growing, ever-evolving mentality. Indeed, it is pleasant to have friends, lovers, family, and such. Just remember that we each must make our own journey in life. Sometimes you have a constant companion for part or most of the way. But eventually, you must go your own separate path. Such is life.

There will be parts of the journey that you have to travel with just yourself as company, and whenever you do, you should try to enjoy yourself and keep moving forward. There is much strength and fortitude to be had by accepting your loneliness as a natural human occurrence and striving through that time that you have to yourself.

MASTERING YOUR EMOTIONS

"Even as rain breaks not through a well-thatched house, passions break not through a well-guarded mind."

—The Pali Tipitaka, *Dhammapada* (Third Century BCE)

In prison, we have an expression called "putting the jumper cables on" someone. Think of the cables you would use to jumpstart a dead car battery. This expression, in prison, is used to describe a form of manipulation. It is primarily done to excite a violent or aggressive response from someone.

Take Shorty, for example. Shorty is known as a decent guy in the prison. Though he doesn't start problems, he always has plenty. Because people know that Shorty has insecurities about his size, they are able to use this knowledge to control his emotions. It does not take much to evoke a violent response from him. All that a person needs to do to put the jumper cables on Shorty is to say, "Hey, Shorty, that guy over there keeps looking at you. He must think you're some kind of clown or something."

Almost immediately, without thinking twice about what he is going to do, Shorty will charge off in the direction of the "offender" and confront him. Usually, it just ends up being a hostile encounter with only words exchanged. Other times, it gets violent, and poor old Shorty gets himself hurt.

As A Prisoner Thinketh

People have tried to talk sense into Shorty. They have also tried to keep people from putting the jumper cables on him, but it is useless. Shorty is a grown man. It is up to him to control his emotions and conquer his insecurities. This is not something that one man can do for another, because it is an internal battle that takes place in the mind. Man is master of, or slave to, his own thoughts and resulting actions or inactions.

Each person must discipline him or herself. If you allow someone to control your thoughts or emotions, then you are essentially allowing that person to control you. Become your own master. Don't let yourself be ruled by emotions. If you allow your emotions to make your decisions, then you will never be in control of yourself. This is what makes highly emotional people so unstable—all it takes is one charged word to set them off. So if the people you are around do not have a good handle on their emotions, you'd be wise to distance yourself from them. Much trouble comes from emotionally based decisions and actions.

Learn how to resist your emotions and others who try to manipulate them. If you can, your life will be much less hectic and chaotic. And you will experience much less pain and fewer negative consequences in the long run.

INFLUENCE

"You know what charm is: a way of getting
the answer yes without having asked
any clear question."

—Albert Camus, *The Fall* (1956)

It seems to me that people generally don't like to feel as if they are being manipulated. Influence, be it intentional or unintentional, happens to be a form of manipulation.

Whether from a stranger, friend, government, political party, or corporation, influence is all around us. Every time we listen to the radio, watch television, talk on our cellular phones, read a book, flip through a magazine, or any number of other activities throughout our day, we are usually being directly influenced or targeted for influence by someone.

Let's look at Jacob. He is a mooch. And his trick to mooching is flattery. He uses compliments to get people's guards down. Then he asks them for food and goods. He is very successful at what he does because he plays off of people's egos and vanity. For instance, he might say something like, "Wow, Robert! Have you been lifting weights, big guy? Because you are really starting to look buff!" Then while our pal Robert is still absorbing the compliment, Jacob will toss in a comment like, "Well, I don't want to keep you from getting to the weight pile so I'm going to go. But before I go, you wouldn't happen to have an extra jar of coffee for a tiny guy like me, would you?"

Surprisingly, a majority of the time, Jacob gets exactly what he has asked for. Not many people

As A Prisoner Thinketh

want to let down the person who makes them feel good about themselves. Jacob is an expert at picking up on people's vanities. He uses charm and flattery to influence them to give him the things that he wants, and he is never short of targets to use his skills on. Instead of realizing that they are being manipulated, people usually just see a nice guy who could use a small favor.

While influence can at times be an inspiring or charismatic creature, it can also be asserted by way of threats, seduction, enticement, and violence. Indeed, there are many forms of delivery. The important thing is to be conscious of outside influence by becoming more aware of the people and environment around us. The more attention you pay to the things that people say and do, the less likely you are to fall victim to their attempts at influencing you.

LEARNING HOW TO TRUST

"Trust not him with your secrets, who, when left alone in the room, turns over your papers."

—Johann Kaspar Lavater, *Aphorisms on Man* (1788)

People would be better off if they were to learn how to trust others.

What exactly is "trust"? Generally speaking, trust is the confidence used to rely on someone or something. The word itself is used too often with very little—or no—clarity, and this ambiguity is what sometimes gets us into trouble with ourselves and others.

Carl B. Brock

Trust can affect our better judgment and cause us to put faith in others when we shouldn't. Whenever we give our trust to someone who didn't deserve it and they go on to break it, ultimately, it's our own faults. While it's *not* our fault that the person we trusted made the choices he did, it *is* our fault because we knew we shouldn't have trusted him in that particular way.

How many times have we smacked our own foreheads and thought, "Man, I knew I shouldn't have loaned him money"? or asked ourselves, "Why did I allow myself to depend on her?" These are perfect examples of paying the price for going against our better judgment.

"Trust" is an overly broad word. It really covers a lot of territory. This is why whenever someone asks if I have trust in another person or thing, I like to inquire, "In what way?" There are many different kinds of trust. For example, there is the trust you have that the babysitter will care for your children in your absence. Another

As A Prisoner Thinketh

example is the trust you have when you ask someone to serve as a job reference. Each one conveys a different type of trust. Trust in one area doesn't necessarily mean trust in another area.

Meet Jeff. He's an easygoing and good-natured guy. Jeff can be trusted to keep his word and is known for conducting business honorably. The only mark against Jeff is that he has a habit of disappearing when things get tough or whenever trouble arises. No one faults Jeff for this—everyone who knows him knows that's just the way he is. All those who know Jeff recognize that if they're in a sticky situation, they shouldn't look to him for backup. Knowing Jeff's tendencies, anyone who turns to him for assistance when they face a grim situation would, unwisely, be expecting him to do something that goes against his nature.

Then there's Gary. While he can always be counted on to have a pal's back in a sticky situation, you'd never want to leave him alone with your wife or girlfriend because he will try to seduce her. This is just how Gary is: that behavior is at the core of his nature.

So you see, the ways to trust are distinguishable from one another. We have a responsibility to ourselves to observe and analyze our friends, family members, and associates. We must identify their characteristics, nature, and beliefs to figure out the particular ways in which we can trust them. To do this, we need to reference their reputations, principles, and past dealings. Above all, we have to be honest with ourselves about who they truly are, as well as what capabilities they do and don't possess.

The world is full of people who have great personalities with very little or no truly good characteristics. Just because someone is funny, exciting, attractive, or charming does not mean they are dependable or trustworthy. For instance, the typical con artist can melt your heart because she tends to be naturally skilled in charming and befriending others to earn their trust.

In order to properly protect ourselves, we must remind ourselves that a person's inherent nature rarely changes. It is highly unlikely that she will treat us differently than the way she has treated everyone else in her life.

I have noticed that many women have the tendency to overlook a man's unfaithful past by telling themselves that he will treat them differently than the way he treated the others. And when the man does what comes naturally to him and cheats on them, these same women curse themselves because they knew that he could not be trusted to remain monogamous, and yet they still did so.

Do not overlook someone's nature. Do not think that you are special or immune to his behavior. Life does not work this way. Going with your instincts may seem like common sense, but sometimes someone's influence can make you forget to listen to your gut.

Let me lay it out for you. If you know that someone is a bad driver, don't loan him your car. If you know someone is a bad worker, don't hire him. If you know someone is irresponsible with money, don't loan him any.

In some cases, you will find a person who can be trusted on multiple levels. This kind of person is worth hanging around. You'd obviously be able to put more trust in this type of person than in others.

Take James, for example. He can be trusted in many ways. His word is good. He does good business. He has respect for other people's relationships. He's a hard worker. He's good with money. And he can be counted on to have your back if you're in a sticky situation. However, James is not good at keeping secrets. If you want to keep something a secret, then you shouldn't tell James. Otherwise, it will most likely be

As A Prisoner Thinketh

revealed. It's not that he intends to break people's confidences, but he just can't help himself because it is in his nature to reveal secrets.

Do yourself a favor and learn how to trust people. Don't use the term too broadly. Try to narrow down the ways in which you trust others. And while you're at it, work on ways in which others can readily trust you.

OVERLOOK THE SMALL STUFF

"The art of being wise is the art of knowing what to overlook."

—William James,
The Principles of Psychology (1890)

The small things in life can add up to be very large things. When it comes to yourself and the way that you live, the best advice is for you to pay attention to the small things that you say and do. However, when it comes to other people, it's best to overlook the small negative things they say or do; this is for your sake rather than theirs.

It seems to me that many people don't put much effort into not offending or irritating others. Many are quite inconsiderate, impolite, and sometimes downright disrespectful.

In society, there is usually a way to leave or distance yourself from an unpleasant person or environment. In prison, there is nowhere to go. Prisoners must try to develop a level of tolerance for people whom they'd never even speak to or come near in society. They are forced to share cells with them, eat meals with them, and work and play with them. There are no breaks or vacations from one another in prison. It only ends when a prisoner is released or dies. If a prisoner were to allow the small things to bother him in here, he'd never have any peace of mind because, rest assured, there will always be someone or something to upset or unnerve him, if he permits it to consume his thoughts and emotions.

As A Prisoner Thinketh

One thing that has always had the capacity to bother me in prison is noise. I've never found unnecessary noise to be pleasant or amusing. Unfortunately, for me, prison is full of noise, and most of it is unnecessary. For example, the slamming of dominoes, the intentional squeaking of shoes, the guards clicking open and shut their empty handcuffs, the amateur rappers banging and drumming on the walls and tables, and the whistling early in the morning or late into the night. The list goes on and on.

I try to remind myself that these people are not making these noises to bother or torture me, personally. In fact, they probably have no clue as to their effect on others. Once I was finally able to accept this, I could more easily focus my attention on other things and ignore those minor nuisances.

If we allow these small negative things to occupy our minds, they will drive us crazy. For our sake, we should ignore them so they do not impact or influence our moods and emotions. Otherwise, we'd never run out of material with which to construct a bad day.

I am sure that everyone has their own irritants and pet peeves. My advice is to not let those things control them, whether through their emotions or actions. In other words, overlook the small stuff.

TAKING ACTION

> "The world is divided into people who do things and people who get the credit. Try, if you can, to belong to the first class. There's far less competition."
>
> —Dwight Morrow, *Letter to Son* (1935)

Plenty of people have great ideas and wonderful aspirations. Many long for something new or hope and wish for change.

The problem is that so few ever seem to take the necessary action required to make any of it come true.

Carl B. Brock

Fear controls many people's lives. And that fear is what keeps most of them from taking action. Sometimes it is a fear of physical injury, but more commonly, it is a fear of mental or emotional pain.

People, in general, are naturally socially driven. They turn to friends and family for encouragement and support. They look to neighbors and strangers for their opinions and views on what is or isn't acceptable, which ends up affecting a person's decision-making process. It causes her to worry too much about what others will say or think. Eventually, the person thinks too long or overanalyzes every step she is considering taking until fear or anxiety sets in. At this point, the dream or goal usually dies.

No one wants to fail. No one wants society to frown on her. Just the mere thought of potential failure is usually all it takes to stop a person right in her tracks. This is why most new things that are achieved are typically done on impulse or in

As A Prisoner Thinketh

a state of strong emotion—usually anger, love, or fear. Indeed, emotions like fear can both compel and inhibit a person from taking action. For instance, a man may dream of traveling abroad for most of his life but never take any of the required actions to do so. Then one day, the man's home country becomes a war zone (think Libya, Syria, or any number of countries at war), and he flees abroad out of fear brought on by the war.

Sure, people will take minor actions throughout the day, but very few people will ever engage in actions that put them outside of their comfort zones. Chuck Palahniuk wrote in his 1996 book *Fight Club*, "It's only after you've lost everything that you're free to do anything." This quote is quite true at an extreme level because, when you have lost everything, you have nothing left to hinder you and thus no longer care about loss or social acceptance. On a less extreme level, which applies in most cases, the person who wishes to do whatever it is he yearns for must get past what it is that inhibits him. To do so, he needs to identify the source of his anxiety, fear, and/or oppression. Next, he must weigh the risk/loss against the reward/gain. If the reward/gain outweighs the risk/loss, then the person can justify the attempt and potential failure to himself if he does not succeed.

However, not every dream or idea should be acted on. The key is to realize that you have it within you to take action, and the wisdom is in the choosing of which action you can take and still be OK with in the event of failure. Not all failure is devastating or destructive. A good amount of failure is healthy and encourages productivity. It teaches us what not to do.

CHOOSE A DIRECTION IN LIFE

> "Two roads diverged in a wood, and I—
> I took the one less traveled by,
> And that has made all the difference."
>
> —Robert Frost, *The Road Not Taken* (1916)

To have a wholesome and meaningful life, it is essential that we each find our own direction. For some people, they must find a new direction because the one in which they were headed has detoured or has reached a dead end. One of the most devastating things that can happen to us is the loss of our purpose—or direction—in life.

I once did time with a man named Matthew. This guy had built his whole existence in society around practicing medicine. He was a family doctor in a small rural town. He loved to help people and was proud of his work. Matthew was a pillar of strength, kindness, and compassion in his community. But like many great men in history, Matthew made some bad choices. The US government deemed these choices to be in violation of federal law and had Matthew prosecuted and sent to prison for many years. As a result, he lost his freedom, his wife, and his career and fell from grace in his close-knit community.

Matthew had become a prisoner just like the rest of us. The only difference was that he hit rock bottom and refused to get back up. He lost all hope. He could not get over the fact that his actions had turned his life upside down. Instead of seeking a new direction and moving forward,

As A Prisoner Thinketh

Matthew gave up. Regrettably, he committed suicide.

Obviously, we need a direction—a sense of purpose—to travel in life. When we live without a sense of purpose, it is hard to put any sincere effort into anything, especially living. But just because life as you know it has lost all of its familiarity does not mean that you can't find a new way to live and keep moving onward.

For some reason, some people are under the illusion that life is supposed to be without pain, tragedy, hardship, failure, loss, embarrassment, and shame. This is a foolish perception that conflicts with reality, and such schools of thought should be abandoned. The truth is that life is full of struggles, error, misfortune, and bad choices. Really, the only difference from one person to the next is the relevancy and scale of these events.

If you are looking for a reason to keep from choosing a direction in life, you will always find one. I've heard just about every response or excuse in some form or another: "I'm afraid," "I'm not smart enough," "I don't have time to learn something new," "I don't know how," "I don't care," "It's not that simple," "My life is over," or "I'm not healthy enough."

We must overcome our own misgivings and lack of motivation. No one can do this for us. This is an internal battle that we must each, as individuals, fight and win alone.

Once we summon the determination and resolve to move forward, we need to choose a direction in which to proceed. It is something to live for, something to dream about, something to care for, something to achieve or accomplish, something or someone to be or become.

There are many paths in life that will take a person in the same direction. For instance, we may wish to become closer to God, so the many paths that could take us in the direction of God could include things like going to church, taking classes in theology, reading and studying

As A Prisoner Thinketh

scripture, or maybe even doing volunteer work. Each are different paths that all head in the same overall direction.

Once you determine your sense of purpose, the paths that take you there will begin to reveal themselves. But before they can appear, you must first find within yourself the overall direction in which you want your life to head. You have to determine this for yourself. Everyone else can only offer helpful advice and suggestions. So do yourself a favor and choose a direction in life.

LIFE-CHANGING EVENTS

"No great improvements in the lot of mankind are
possible, until a great change takes place
in the fundamental constitution
of their modes of thought."

—John Stuart Mill, *Autobiography* (1873)

I have a theory about why so few people ever succeed in changing who they are. People are creatures of habit, and this obviously is a big part of it. But when you get down to the core of it, people only change when either they feel like they have to or when something has happened that makes them feel as if they can never be the same again.

For the typical person, discipline is hard work. Whenever he gets into a situation that requires discipline in order for him to change, it is unlikely that he will see it through, whereas the people who do change after some significant event seem to have a better chance at success. This type of phenomenon is known as a Life-Changing Event.

A Life-Changing Event is something that changes our inner belief systems, shocks our consciousness, or touches our emotions on a very deep level. The peculiar thing about these events is that, while one incident may be a genuine Life-Changing Event for one person, that same thing may not cause another person to even consider changing. Things affect everyone differently.

A good example of a Life-Changing Event for most people is to have a Near-Death Experience. A Near-Death Experience is pretty self-explanatory:

As A Prisoner Thinketh

it's an experience that brings a person close to death.

My example of a Near-Death Experience that also happens to be a Life-Changing Event is what happened to a teenager named Amy. One night, while returning home from work, Amy allowed herself to be distracted by her cellular phone while she was driving. The result was a bad car wreck that landed her in the local hospital with serious injuries. Once Amy recovered from surgery and realized what had happened, she vowed never to use a cellular phone while driving again. For Amy, the accident was a Life-Changing Event. For another person it may not have been. It just depends on the person. Plenty of things can be Life-Changing Events: the death of a loved one, a birth, a Near-Death Experience, newfound religion, a spiritual journey/awakening, jail/prison time, and so forth.

Something that does not ordinarily strike me as a Life-Changing Event is marriage, at least not in America. It just doesn't have the aspects of a Life-Changing Event, which may explain why so many people in the United States are divorced. Commonly, people go on to marry someone who is not right for him or her because either the person he or she married was hiding his or her true identity until after the marriage or one partner, unwisely, thought that marriage would change his or her mate into something better. However, marriage, for the most part, is little more than a change in titles, not mentalities. Saying "I do" does not, itself, change a bad boyfriend into a good husband, nor does it transform a bad girlfriend into a good wife.

For some people—and very few at that—jail and/or prison time can be a Life-Changing Event. But as I said, I must admit that it is quite rare, and this is probably why recidivism rates are so high. For something to have the potential to become a Life-Changing Event, it must really shock the consciousness or stir up something

As A Prisoner Thinketh

deep within a person's emotions. It is usually the guys in prison who have a very tough time adjusting to their situation who encounter a real Life-Changing experience. Every once in a while, you see a guy who adjusted well but eventually got sick and tired of his lifestyle and its consequences and decides to change. This, too, is a Life-Changing Event because he allowed his circumstances to touch his emotions on a very deep level.

In the end, I believe that people who change had it in them all along. The Life-Changing Event just kind of pushed them over the edge.

SPIRITUAL JOURNEYS

"A man travels the world over in search of what he needs and returns home to find it."

—George Moore, *The Brook Kerith* (1916)

I used to wonder why people went on self-declared Spiritual Journeys. I think I understand now.

It seems to me that we all need something different in life to fill that void or satisfy the emptiness/loneliness that we as humans so often feel. I suppose that the problem is that many people don't have the luxury of sitting around and figuring out what it is they need or want in order to feel happy and complete in this life. If everyone had this extra time to spare to just sit and ponder, I am sure that most would see they already have everything they need. A great many of the rest would be able to see what actions they need to take to obtain their innermost desires.

So when a person does finally set out on a Spiritual Journey, whether it be via physical, mental, or both means, this person is making a type of personal declaration to put his current life on hold in order to examine or reexamine his direction and course of travel, so to speak. This is what makes a Spiritual Journey such a Life-Changing Event. The person who embarks on it is actually deciding, on a deep level, whether to continue down the path he is headed or to change course. In essence, this person is determining whether he should change his inner belief system, aspirations, lifestyle, and/or principles, all of

As A Prisoner Thinketh

which affect his personhood and future choices.

Sometimes, in order to appreciate the things that we deem to be small or of little importance, we have to go without them for a period of time. To do so, we leave our usual comfort zone and everything familiar to us in order to see our life from a different perspective.

FIND A MENTOR

"Listen to counsel, receive instruction,
and accept correction that you may be wise
in the time to come."

—Proverbs 19:20, *Amplified Bible*

Most of us have heard the expression "There's an easy way and a hard way." This is typically said with regard to the learning process. Generally speaking, this expression means that we can either learn a lesson on our own (the hard way) or learn from someone who already possesses the knowledge (the easy way). It is no secret that many children grow up without parents in their lives or have ones who didn't make much of a difference. It is my opinion that whenever a child grows up without effective parental role models or mentors, he or she misses out on critical knowledge and advice about life lessons and social skills. These children are forced to try new things alone without any guidance and thus learn the hard way through their own failures and successes.

Sometimes, everything turns out OK for the child. Other times a parent, aunt or uncle, neighbor, schoolteacher, coach, or grandparent picks up the extra slack and helps the child along his or her way. But a lot of the time, the parentless child makes some very unwise choices and develops the habit of making poor decisions. As a result, the child gets stuck in a cycle of calamity, tragedy, and despair of his or her own creation. This usually continues into adulthood and becomes a defining factor in his or her life. It is not surprising that this road usually leads to addiction, disease, jail/prison, and early death.

As A Prisoner Thinketh

Indeed, no one makes you choose right or wrong, yes or no, or true or false, just as no one is responsible for your ultimate success, failure, awards, or losses. We, as individuals, make our own destiny and are the sole masters of our predicaments. The point here is that each of us, whether we are a child or an adult, is much better off when we make informed decisions rather than relying on guesswork or chance. Maybe better-informed people will make the same choices in the end, but at least they possess the knowledge to better understand the ultimate consequences of those choices.

We are all better served when we have someone to learn from. Just as a tour guide can show us around a new city, a mentor can give us insight and advice on certain subjects, thoughts, and skills. In school, a child typically learns mathematics from a math teacher, science from a science teacher, and English from an English teacher. Sometimes there is one teacher who teaches all of these subjects and more, but usually it is an individual teacher for each subject. Mentors are similar in this way. For example, if a person wanted to learn how to drive a vehicle and how to work on and repair automotive engines, he probably would not have much difficulty finding someone who could teach him both skills. But let's say that he wanted to learn how to sail a boat or how to build houses. These are very different skills that would likely require him to find separate teachers.

Mentors are one of the best teaching resources. They can show us shortcuts and point out pitfalls. When choosing a mentor, we should be certain that we are choosing wisely. It is not good to learn from someone who does things incorrectly or who has a poor reputation, because the pupil could waste time learning the wrong way to do something.

To me, the most important kind of mentor is the one who helps us find out who we are and points us in the right direction for our personal journey. This type of mentor is the one who shows us how to treat others, how to make better choices, how to define our principles, how to find our aspirations, and what to look for in others when making friends and choosing lovers. Some of the most important lessons in life involve love, friendship, family, wealth, health, and spirituality. A good mentor can teach us what he or she has learned about any one of these subjects. By doing so, the mentor can help shape our mentalities and inner beliefs.

Just like any other teacher, a mentor is supposed to be a sort of guide. If you disagree with the mentor or find some area of conflict or contradiction in his or her statements, advice, or principles, then you can always ignore, challenge, or disagree with those opinions and refuse to accept or apply them, if need be.

Mentors are not perfect. No one is. But mentors can make the learning process much easier and less painful.

HOPE KEEPS THE SPIRIT ALIVE

"After all, tomorrow is another day."

—Margaret Mitchell, *Gone with the Wind* (1936)

I t seems to me that the people who have the strongest hope also have the strongest spirits. I believe that they go hand in hand.

Hope keeps the spirit alive, and when there is no hope, the spirit disappears.

I know that my hope is what has carried me through my darkest days in prison. There have been times when I have been on the brink of giving up my hope for a good future, and they were the lowest parts of my existence. Fortunately, I never completely gave up hope. I found strength in myself to persevere. I fought hard during those times to keep my hope and spirit intact. I knew that if I ever completely gave up hope, my life would be over.

In order to maintain a grip on that ledge I dangled from, I had to reinforce my constitution with visions and dreams of a future freedom full of peace and happiness. Oftentimes, it seemed as though I was fighting a never-ending war within myself. This internal struggle left me tired and weak to the point of mental and physical exhaustion. The only thing that saw me through my pain, loneliness, torment, and despair was a distant hope, itself abstract and almost nonexistent.

But the peculiar thing I've discovered about hope is that if it does not grow weaker, it will certainly grow stronger. My hope had gotten as

As A Prisoner Thinketh

low and weak as I could possibly allow it to go. And then it leveled off. I had hit rock bottom.

Yet even at the bottom, I refused to completely give up. Once I acknowledged my final resolve, my hope began to grow stronger. My visions and dreams of the future began to take shape, and I was able to see possibilities and potential realities in my heart and mind. Then my hope became strong and durable. I was able to hold it with conviction because I learned to believe in myself, and that is when my hope became something real to me. It wasn't real in the physical sense, but in the spiritual sense. My spirit was full of vitality and bursting at the seams with energy. I then had motivation, clearer thoughts, and positive emotions. My hope in the future allowed me to let go of my dark past, endure the harsh present, and move toward the future with peace of mind.

I have been inspired by many people. But one person I met in prison stands out among the rest with regard to hope. His name is Paul.

Carl B. Brock

Paul is a good friend of mine. He and I were cellmates in a maximum-security federal prison. Paul is what you'd call a reformed escape artist. He has spent decades in prison: he is currently serving a 155-year sentence in the federal prison system.

Paul originally went to state prison in Arizona for some minor offenses about four decades ago. While doing time there, he decided that he'd rather not be incarcerated. So Paul devised an elaborate escape that started with his faking a snakebite and being taken to a local emergency room for treatment. Once he was at the hospital, which was a less secure building, he made his escape and went on the run. While Paul was on the lam, he robbed some federally insured banks, got busted at some point afterward, and was returned to federal prison, and he has remained there since the 1970s. During his lengthy stay, he has tried many elaborate methods of escape—everything from sawing off window bars and

As A Prisoner Thinketh

making a homemade ladder to scale a wall to attempting to climb a guard tower (which he fell from).

Paul is definitely a free spirit. He is highly intelligent and very down-to-earth. He has an amiable nature with a very big heart. No matter how much time he is serving, no matter how bad the prison conditions are, Paul remains hopeful. He hopes for freedom. He eats, sleeps, and breathes freedom. Thoughts of freedom are what keep Paul's spirit alive.

Fortunately for him, the US Parole Commission has finally given him a parole date some four-plus decades after first being incarcerated.

As I said, Paul stood out to me. I'm not saying that he is the only guy in prison who hopes for freedom—far from it. All that I am saying is that he truly lives for it. And by doing so, Paul has freedom in his mind, heart, and most importantly, his spirit. If you look closely at Paul, you can see it and feel it radiating from him. This is Paul's vitality: this is what keeps him going. And if you saw it, you'd probably be inspired, too.

So don't let go of your hope. Don't give up on what keeps you going. If you lose hope for one thing, then try to replace it with hope for something else. I can assure you that hope is what keeps the spirit alive—and the spirit is what keeps us going.

RESULTS

Carl B. Brock
(2015)

Where there is a Dream,
there is a Hope.

Where there is a Hope,
there is a Will.

Where there is a Will,
there is a Possibility.

Where there is a Possibility,
there is a Choice.

Where there is a Choice,
there is an Action.

Where there is an Action,
there are Results.

ACKNOWLEDGMENTS

"The Lord is my Strength and my [impenetrable] Shield; my heart trusts in, relies on, and confidently leans on Him, and I am helped; therefore my heart greatly rejoices, and with my song will I praise Him."

—Psalm 28:7, *Amplified Bible*

First and foremost, I'd like to thank the Lord for the strength He has given me, the lessons He has seen me through, and His never-ending blessings. With Him, all things are possible. Thank you.

Next, I'd like to thank my mother—thanks,

Carl B. Brock

Mom—family, and friends for their love, support, dedication, and patience. Without you I'd be in bad shape. I need all the help I can get, and you have helped me a lot. Thank you.

Last, but not least, I'd like to salute the late, but not forgotten, James Allen. You, sir, were and remain, one of the greatest thinkers of all time. I am very thankful to have stumbled across the precious writings you left behind. Your works have changed my entire thought process. As a result, you've changed my choices and direction in life. Thank you.

Sincerely,

Carl B. Brock

ABOUT THE AUTHOR

"The man who makes no mistakes
usually does not make anything."

—Edward John Phelps, *Speech* (1889)

Carl B. Brock is currently serving a seventeen-year sentence in federal prison for the distribution of the chemical substance MDMA, or ecstasy.

Shortly after his incarceration, Carl began a continuous and ever-evolving study of religion, politics, language, science, music, law, and philosophy. He has since written numerous songs and poems and is currently working on several manuscripts (both fiction and nonfiction). Carl is

Carl B. Brock

enrolled in college and is pursuing his bachelor's degree in business, which he plans to obtain before his release from prison.

For more about Carl, please visit
www.AsAPrisonerThinketh.com

www.ingramcontent.com/pod-product-compliance
Lightning Source LLC
Chambersburg PA
CBHW071304040426
42444CB00009B/1866